I0461765

25 reasons why selling sucks and 25 ways you can make it suck less.

An honest approach to the ugliness of sales.

Published by Timothy E. Borthwick
ISBN 978-0-359-83982-7

Contents

Introduction

Selling sucks. It has to be one of the most difficult jobs to take. But why are some able to do is so well and for so long while others give up so quickly or can't perform at the level required of them? Selling a product or service is a skill, that once you master can open many doors and financial opportunity for you. In this book we are going to dive into 25 reasons why selling sucks and 25 ways it can suck less. By understanding these 25 points with exercises you can do or think about to overcome these barriers then it will help create success if done correctly over time.

Now please understand, there isn't going to be lengthy chapters filled with fluff. I want to get right to the point on how we can overcome what sucks and start creating success in sales.

Focus on what I provide as a solution and make an effort to apply it everyday in the field and when you have some down time.

Many of us are not naturally talented when it comes to selling. Most of us have to work hard at it and continue to work at it over an extended period of time. This is the process. Things do not just happen overnight. The harder you work at your career and mastering the skills to accomplish what is necessary than the sooner you will live the life you desire.

If selling is what you currently do, want to do or are thinking about doing then you need to go all in. You can not be a half ass salesperson and expect desirable results. There are areas that you need to become great in order to sustain a financial future in sales but also remain happy with what you're doing. If you spend your entire career struggling and not improving your skills then you will fail or become miserable with what it is you're doing. Become great or work at becoming great and certain things that suck for you now wont suck in the future. Are you ready for things to start sucking less? Let's begin.

1. It's Hard

Selling is hard. It's hard approaching a stranger and trying to get them to buy your product. It's hard to make a phone call and getting hit with rejection. It's hard plain and simple. If selling was easy wouldn't everyone do it? It's a career that pays well if you can handle it but if it were easy more people would do it. Sales is hard because it requires dedication, practice and the will to make money.

What are you doing to make things easier? Are you putting in the necessary time both at work and at home? Are you educating yourself or connecting with top sales people who you can learn from? See if you're not doing what's necessary than it will always be hard. Preparation by repetition over time allows things to become easier. Developing skills will make things easier.

How can things become easier?

Repetition.

Ongoing training or self education.

Connecting with sales people more skilled than you to find out what they do.

Spend more time on your career and less time on leisure. If you want things to be easier than you need to become better. Do you know who said that? It's Jim Rohn, a master salesperson. It could be a good start for you to start studying him.

2. Rejection Sucks

No matter who throws rejection your way it sucks. The girl or guy you like denied you when you asked them out? Did you stop trying? Did you stop seeking sex or a significant other because you got rejected? I doubt it. The first time we were rejected by anyone was most likely in this situation yet people never give up on finding someone else. They have to reproduce, have sex and feel someone next to them at night.

You could approach sales the same way. You got rejected but why do you think the next person will reject you. There's always a buyer of what it is you're selling. Rejection only gets easier through repetition and understanding rejection is just part of the process. It will always exist for those pursuing a career in sales. Anticipate that it will happen, but do not let it consume you. Never let one rejection let you think that everyone will reject you. Rejection is an opportunity to learn and will help you build some thick skin.

How to handle rejection
- **Don't overthink it**
- **Embrace it but don't let it consume you**
- **Learn from it**
- **Practice your pitch. Remember, repetition and preparation**

3. People who don't sell for a living hate you

Sometimes it feels like people cast you out when you're a salesperson. Do you have people like that around you? Maybe friends or family tell you to get a "steady job" or maybe they spend less time with you for fear that you'll try to sell them something? This usually happens to network marketers or salespeople who sell a consumer product.

People may have this weird vibe towards you if you're in sales or have tried selling them something in the past. This is something I dislike about network marketing, MLM or small sales companies that want you to start by pitching your friends or family. If you can try to avoid this or strictly use it for practice. At all costs avoid selling to friends and family if you wish to hold onto these relationships. A good company who believes in their products and their training wouldn't put you through that or force it on you.

4. Job Security

The task of sales is selling. You're hired to perform and unfortunately when you don't perform the company will can you. This shouldn't come as a surprise. Sales is something I've always hated but it's also the only type of job I've ever had. Some things that are crucial when you're starting out or even struggling in sales is becoming coachable and being present. Let me explain.

Creating job security in sales

- **Be coachable (Listen and do)**
- **Be present (Show up everyday. Be early too)**
- **Be likeable (People like you then they will vouch for you or want to help you)**
- **Voice what you're struggling with before your boss does (Let your boss know "Hey im struggling, what can I do differently?")**

- Ask questions
- Make yourself useful in other ways (How can I help?)
- Work hard (Your manager and team will help someone who works hard)

These are just some things you can do when you're struggling to help extend your job security but also help you get out of your slump. Remember, in sales selling is everything. Performance= termination or promotion. Which will it be for you?

5. Paid To Perform

When you work in a salaried position then you know that you get the same paycheck every

Friday without question. You come in, clock-in, perform your tasks and clock- out. But in sales you have to make things happen. You have to acquire new customers or get old customers to buy if you want to eat. Paying your bills, putting gas in your car, and even keeping a roof over your head all comes down to your performance.

I know these things weigh heavily on you. Sometimes you're freaking out, wondering if you'll make the money you need to make this month. Once you get in that mindset it might start to feel like all you're getting is rejection. No sales, no leads and just a mindful of stress.

Start focusing less on the pain lack of sales will bring, but start thinking about the joy it will bring to yourself and the ones you love. You need to have a goal mindset and not a fear of failure mindset. Focus on big goals you want to achieve rather than simply making rent. You've made rent payments in the past. If you're goal is to only make rent and pay bills then you'll most likely fall short. MAke your goals bigger. You'll work harder to attain them and the smaller goals will be automatic.

6. Success depends on the prospects decision to buy

Your success depends on someone's decision to buy what it is you're selling. Having money or being broke depends on that one thing in sales. But that's not the prospects fault. Their decision to buy depends on how persuasive you were. How knowledgeable were you on the product? Did you listen to their objections? Did you ask enough questions? It all comes down to you. Some people will just say no and never buy. Most people will buy but you need to do your job. This all comes down to you and the time you spend mastering the skills necessary to overcome objections and be the great salesperson you were meant to be.

Work hard at the skills necessary to create success. Do not blame a prospect for what you lack.

7. The Quota

Sales metrics are the worst. Usually right after your probationary period you'll have to start hitting your quota every month. Just what you need, more added pressure. You are paid to perform. You are paid to grow the company. When you don't grow the company then your employer can't pay you.

Your quota is going to scare you when you're falling short. That's usually what scares salespeople is the idea of falling short on the quota. But why do you fall short? You are chasing the target. If you're required to make 30 sales a month and only have 20 sales then that means you're falling short based on what you're putting into your efforts.

What would happen if you raised your target from 30 to 50? Well the first thing you would need to do is work nearly twice as hard to reach the goal of 50 sales. Doubling your target takes more effort and time but if you fall short do you think you'll hit your quota? Sales is a ruthless game and consumes a lot of your time in the early years. Hitting your quota requires increased effort, consistency and drive. Set big goals and raise your target.

8. The customer thinks you're sleazy

You've probably had a customer tell you they're not interested, not to call again, put me on the do not call list, etc. They don't want you to call, they don't want to deal with you and they don't care what you're selling. They were sold in the past and felt like they were taken advantage of. That's a normal reaction.

We want to protect ourselves. We don't want to buy something we don't need or currently in the market for. We especially don't want some salesman coming in selling us something while they get richer. People think this way and they have every right to. But you as the salesperson can't go in thinking everyone already dislikes you because you want to sell them something.

Some things you can do as a salesperson to prevent the hate towards you by the prospect is qualify the customer. See we all want to sell by explaining features or benefits. But did you even qualify the prospect first? Did you ask them questions to first gather if this is even right for them? See when you qualify a prospect first it gives you a chance to first have a conversation, ask questions and ease in the product rather than just jamming it down the prospects throat.

When you want to help people rather than sell people it will show. When you know your product or service can help someone and you've qualified them first. I guarantee you'll have a better chance at closing the deal and the prospect liking you and will appreciate you.

9. Selling Is Repetitive

Doing the same thing everyday, over and over again. Selling can be repetitive. It's one thing that really sucks about doing it. Most jobs can be repetitive. Here are some things that can help relieve that.

1. Show a personality. Get the prospect to laugh and have fun whether on the phone or in person. Being flat and boring will just drive your crazy and make you hate what you do.
2. Change up your schedule. Don't always keep things the same.
3. When you hit a goal create another goal. Once you have achieved what it is you want to achieve you need to set new goals to keep yourself chasing something. If not what's the point?

10. Dealing With No

Dealing with no is the same thing as what we discussed about rejection. It's part of the job and it comes with the territory. Overcome it by being prepared and embracing that sometimes the answer is just no.

Preparation through repetition = less no more yes

11. Selling the same thing over and over again sucks

Selling the same thing over and over again goes hand and hand with the repetitive nature of sales. Everyday making calls pitching the same pitch over and over again on the same product or service. How boring can that get? This is just part of the job again. Not much you can do here. But you can change up your pitch. Changing up your pitch can help mix things up but if you have a pitch that's working then you might not want to change it.

Once you have your pitch down and feel you don't want to change it then become an expert of the product or service you are selling. When you know all there is to know on what it is you're selling then you'll enjoy it more. You'll be comfortable having conversations about it. When you are comfortable things suck less.

12. Engaging the prospect

I like sales because its almost a competition between you and the prospect. One person is going to fold and give up or give in. When you stop engaging with the prospect you will lose. When the prospect hasn't agreed to buy yet and you stop engaging then the prospect has let go of the hook. Keep the customer or prospect engaged at all times. Shut up and listen. When you're done with your pitch ask questions. Questions will keep them engaged and help them open up. It gives you time to stop talking and develop a strategy to circle back and touch on the pain point or something that they had just expressed. An answer to your question is another opportunity to close.

13. Appearance

Sometimes someone will look right at you before opening your mouth and judge you. Appear clean and confident. When you look good, you feel good. Keep a clean and appropriate appearance. When you don't feel good your performance will suffer greatly. This doesn't mean you should roll up in a fancy car wearing designer clothes. You need to embrace your audience and dress accordingly. But your appearance is a representation of you. So dress as if your job depended on it.

14. Public Speaking

No arguing that this one sucks. It sucked in school and it sucks now. It's scary to get up in front of people and look confident when on the inside you're a ton of nerves. Whether it's on the phone, in person or in front of multiple people speaking in a professional manner to a stranger that you're trying to close is a hard thing to do.

This is not something that comes natural to the majority of people. It's something most will avoid at all costs and it's something you might struggle with or dislike entirely. But we can all agree that if you want to work in sales than its not going anywhere and you better suck it up and learn to deal with it.

The fear of the phone or the crowd comes from the same place ive been talking about over and over again. Ready? The answer is preparation and repetition. When you're prepared with what it is you're presenting and when you've done it more times than you can count the fear will eventually subside. The nerves may always be there but understand that the nerves are putting your body in a state of readiness. So when you're nervous just know its your body getting you ready to be prepared.

15. Long Hours

Long hours are the worst. You get up in the morning and it's dark and you get home after dark. Some days never seeing any daylight because during those hours you're stuck behind a desk pumping out calls.

For some this causes fights with a spouse that lead to divorce or troubled marriages. Long hours make you feel like all you do is work and never enjoy life. I know it feels like this at times. I've been there.

You don't want to do the long hours forever. First identify what's causing the long hours. If you're not hitting your target and forced to stay late to meet your quota then you're not prepared. You're lacking somewhere. Or it could be the repetition. Either way you should understand that sales isn't a life sentence, but to be great you have to invest the time. This could mean weekends working on your skills or even after work. Sales is a career that can open many doors for you but you need to do what it takes. Long hours is sometimes part of the process. Do not neglect your family or spouse in order to reach your goals. Instead of TV or Leisure time spend that time working on yourself and your career.

16. Handling Objections

Who the hell wants to do this? Someone says no thank you, most of the time I just want to say "no problem have a good day". I can't say that, if I did I would be homeless. Handling objections is a hard thing to do. Why can't the prospect just say yes? If all you're after is the sale then you're going to struggle if sales doesn't come natural to you. Be an ambassador of the product or service you sell. Make the prospect understand that you're fully behind your product and you want them to know about it. Help them understand you care about their needs by asking them questions and letting them talk. You're qualifying the prospect and getting them to explain why your product can help them.

Objections will always exist in sales. It's a natural human response. It needs to come natural to you to show you're thinking about the prospect and their best interest. Some just won't buy and that's ok. Other's need to know

you're certain that they need to buy from you.

You need to make them certain as well. Get

people to agree with you and agree with them

and the objection will be easier to overcome.

17. High Risk

Selling is a risky game to play. The fear of

job security when missing your quota or the

potential of a buyout or merger can be scary.

Most of the time you're just looked at as a

number in sales. Especially if you're an average

or below average performer. We all know that

sales guy who outperforms everyone and gets

special treatment. They exist in all companies. But remember one thing. That salesperson created that opportunity for themselves and you can do it too.

You're fear is most likely coming from your lack of effort or laziness. If you stopped caring or leave early when you should be staying later than there is no one to blame except for yourself. If you have done everything you can. You stay late, you ask questions, you read and self educate yourself on your own time and apply it but you're still no good at sales than maybe it's not for you. But it's extremely rare that someone puts in that much effort and can't see some results.

Your fear of job security comes from your insecurity on your efforts and laziness. Change those two things and the fear will be minimal.

18. Training

Training can suck. Reading, reviewing and applying isn't ideal and it can be boring. Training is your key to success. When you work for a company that has ongoing training that means they care about the success of their sales staff. They want you to succeed and when you succeed they succeed. The training you do on your own is where the magic happens. When it's after hours and you're putting in the time that is where you will see the growth. Let's say you have two athletes. Both are talented but one stays for 3 hours after every practice to shoot free throws. Who's going to be better in a year? This is the same thing for everything. If you want to thrive and be successful than you need to become obsessed with all aspects including training.

19. This job is becoming boring

You're not setting new goals. You're not mixing things up. You're not working towards becoming the best version of yourself. You're trying to survive rather than thrive. That is how things become boring. Change your mindset, your goals and increase effort.

20. The Commitment

You make commitments. You committed to your spouse, your kids, even yourself. Why are you not committed to your career? It goes hand and hand with being committed to all of those things above. How can you provide for the people you care about when you can't commit to being the best version of you at work or at home? Step up and do what it takes. When you're lacking in anything it's because you haven't committed to doing what's required of you to have excess. When you're sucking at work or as a husband it's because you're not doing what is necessary for both of those things. Sometimes this means getting to the office at 6am to do what it takes so you can be home by 5pm to spend time with your family. Commitment requires sacrifice. Are you willing to make a sacrifice?

21. Low Starting Pay

Sales usually means low starting salary or base pay when you first start. The big money is in the commissions and the base is looked at as a safety net to keep employees hanging on. It really sucks in the beginning. You're learning how to sell or getting the pitch down and making about $500 a week before taxes. It feels like you would be better off flipping burgers, less stress and more time for you.

This is something all sales people suffer through in the beginning. Your base should not be looked at as your pay. If anything it should motivate you to make the sales you need to make. If you're bitching about the low base pay then you're in the wrong place. Keep your eyes on the prize. Get great and make some freaking sales!

22. The Boss

Your job sucks, the pay sucks, and the prospect sucks. You come to work and now even the boss is coming down on you. He expresses how you didn't make your quota last month. You're phone time is low or your not handling objections well. You don't want to hear this if anything you want to quit right then and there.

Your boss or managers have a job to do. They have a quota to meet and they need to have certain expectations in order for things to get done. They should want you to be successful and you should too. You should be able to talk to them and get help from them or your team. If you work in a place where they don't want to help you then you should find a place that will. If you don't want to help yourself then it could be time for a career change because you're checked out.

23. Growth Potential

You can become a very successful individual in sales without having to move up the ladder or take on a leadership role. But for some, they want to move up the ladder and want to feel as though they hold a position with more value than just being a sales rep. This can be difficult in a small sales company or even corporate sales. I am not saying it's impossible but it can be difficult. If that is what you're seeking then express it. If you have already expressed it and was told "not now" or "We will look at promotion opportunities at a later time" then you need to put yourself in position to become more valuable. Show people how you can fill a position that you want to hold.

Growth = becoming the best version of you + massive exposure

24. Competition

There are two types of competition that are going to exist in sales. It's the direct competition with other companies and the internal competition you have with other sales people. Get rid of both. The only competition that should exist is with yourself. Everyday you should focus on you and only worry about competing with who you were yesterday.

When it comes to direct competition with other companies do not bad mouth or insult what they do. Show the prospect how you differ but be professional. Don't focus on them as it can come off as being insecure. Vouch for your product and show them how it can help them. Do not spend an ounce of time bad mouthing or degrading anyone or any company.

You are the competition. Be better than yesterday.

25. Customer Service

What sucks more than sales? Customer service does. They get yelled at for things that went wrong with the customers experience all day everyday. They show up and do it the next day. But sometimes the sales person needs to be a customer service agent. You should always be looking to serve the customer. Being strong in customer service and showing empathy when things go wrong for them is as important as the sale. Care about your customer. Customer service goes a long way when you're only paid to be a salesperson.

Wrapping Things Up

I hope you didn't expect any secrets in this book. I actually hope you say "No shit, I know all of this already". I Want people to understand that every career can suck. Selling most definitely sucks. But through repetition and preparation it can suck less. Be great at what you do. Be so good that when someone asks you questions you just answer so naturally. Sales is comprised of multiple components that you need to understand and become great at in order to reach the success and happiness you're striving for.

Things begin to suck less when you realize that these things will always exist but you have the ability to make the best of the situation. Everyday you have the chance to be the best version of you. You are in control. Take control of what sucks in your life by being ready, being focused and being certain. Selling sucks, but

you don't have to.

www.ingramcontent.com/pod-product-compliance
Lightning Source LLC
Chambersburg PA
CBHW061227180526
45170CB00003B/1190